paperblanks®
PARISIAN MOSAIC

Notre collection Mosaïque Parisienne s'inspire d'une reliure en cuir mosaïque du XVIIIe siècle réalisée à Paris par le maître-relieur Nicolas-Denis Derome. Issu d'une célèbre famille de relieurs, son travail était très prisé car il offrait un style unique de légèreté et de vivacité du motif.
Cette couverture polychromatique et dorée rappelle un motif médiéval appelé « au semé », lequel se compose de petits motifs décoratifs disposés en lignes ou colonnes symétriques, tel un champ cousu. L'adoption de cet ancien motif héraldique associé à des couleurs originales et de nouvelles matières transporte la reliure mosaïque vers une nouvelle ère artistique.

Unsere Kollektion „Pariser Mosaik" wurde durch einen ledernen Mosaikeinband aus dem 18. Jahrhundert inspiriert, den der großartige Buchbinder Nicolas-Denis Derome gefertigt hat. Die Arbeiten des Meisters, der aus einer berühmten Familie von Buchbindern stammt, waren sehr begehrt, weil sie von einzigartigem Gespür für leichte und lebendige Designs zeugten.
Dieser mit Gold geschmückte und vielfarbige Einband erinnert an ein mittelalterliches Motiv, *au semé* genannt, das aus kleinen dekorativen Mustern besteht, die in symmetrischen Linien oder Reihen angeordnet sind, was einem gesäten Feld ähnelt. Die Übernahme dieses alten heraldischen Motivs, verbunden mit dem Gebrauch von frischen Farben und neuen Materialien, brachte den Mosaikeinband in eine neue Ära der Kunstfertigkeit.

La nostra collezione Mosaico Parigino è ispirata ad una rilegatura in pelle con mosaico incastonato del XVIII secolo, eseguita a Parigi dal maestro Nicolas-Denis Derome. Discendente da una rinomata famiglia di rilegatori, i lavori di Derome furono molto ricercati per il loro stile vivace e dalla inconfondibile leggerezza.
Questa copertina policromatica decorata in oro si rifà al *au semé*, un soggetto medioevale che consiste in un accurato elemento decorativo disposto su linee simmetriche che ricordano i solchi di un campo seminato. L'adozione di questo antico motivo araldico accostato a vividi colori e a nuovi materiali, ha proiettato la rilegatura con mosaico in una nuova sfera dell'arte.

Nuestra colección Mosaico Parisino se inspira en una encuadernación en mosaico en piel realizada en París en el siglo XVIII por el maestro encuadernador Nicolas-Denis Derome. Las obras de Derome, quien provenía de una renombrada familia de encuadernadores, eran muy solicitadas por su estilo único lleno de ligereza y vivacidad.
Esta cubierta policromada y repujada en oro recuerda un motivo medieval llamado *au semé*, caracterizado por pequeños motivos decorativos dispuestos en líneas o columnas simétricas a modo de campo sembrado. La adopción de este antiguo motivo heráldico combinado con colores vivos y nuevos materiales llevó la encuadernación en mosaico a una nueva era artística.

「パリのモザイク」は、18世紀のパリで製本の名手Nicolas-Denis Deromeが手がけたモザイク文様の皮革装丁を再現。製本で名高い一族出身のDeromeの作品は、粋な軽さと快活なデザインで知られ、人気を博しました。
金箔押しに多色使いの装丁は、縦横対称に細かい装飾を直線にちりばめ、播種された畑にも似た中世のモチーフ「au semé」を思わせます。この旧き紋章モチーフが新鮮な色彩と素材に出会い、モザイク装丁に新たな芸術の時代が訪れました。

1103203

paperblanks®
PARISIAN MOSAIC

Mosaïque

Our Parisian Mosaic cover was inspired by an eighteenth-century leather mosaic binding executed in Paris by master binder Nicolas-Denis Derome. Descended from a renowned family of bookbinders, his works were much sought after as they showed a unique flair for lightness and vivacity of design.

This gold-tooled and polychromatic cover recalls a mediæval motif called *au semé*, which consists of small decorative patterns arranged in symmetrical lines or columns resembling a sown field. The adoption of this ancient heraldic motif, combined with fresh colours and new materials, brought mosaic binding into a new era of artistry.

ISBN: 978-1-4397-1684-7
MIDI FORMAT   144 PAGES   LINED
DESIGNED IN CANADA